MW01614719

Contributions of the Muslim Woman in Giving Sincere Advice

SHAYKH DOCTOR RIḌĀ BIN KHĀLID BŪSHĀMAH

© Maktabatulirshad Publications, USA

All rights reserved. No part of this publication may be reproduced in any language, stored in any retrieval system or transmitted in any form or by any means, whether electronic, mechanic, photocopying, recording or otherwise, without the express permission of the copyright owner.

ISBN: 978-1-9442-4787-4

First Edition: Rabī' Thānī 1437 A.H. / February 2016 C.E.

Cover Design: Maktabatulirshad staff

Translation by ʿAbdullāh Omrān

Revision & Editing by Maktabatulirshad staff

Typesetting & formatting by Abū Sulaymān Muhammad ʿAbdul-ʿAẓīm Ibn Joshua Baker

Printing: Ohio Printing

Subject: Women/ Advice

Website: www.maktabatulirshad.com

E-mail: info@maktabatulirshad.com

فهرس

Table of Contents

BRIEF BIOGRAPHY OF THE AUTHOR

He is Shaykh Doctor Abū ʿAbdul-Bārī Riḍā bin Khālid Būshāmah, the Salafi Shaykh. He has numerous great works. He was born on November 29th, 1968 in Algiers, the capital of Algeria.

His scholarly qualifications:

- Bachelor's degree in Islāmic sciences with excellence; major of the Prophetic Ḥadīth. He was awarded his degree from the Faculty of Ḥadīth and Islāmic studies., Islāmic University in Madīnah 1415 A.H. (1994 C.E.).
- Master's degree in the Islāmic sciences with excellence; major of Ḥadīth sciences from the faculty of Ḥadīth and Islāmic studies., Islāmic University in Madīnah 1420 A.H. (2000 C.E.).
- A Ph.D. in Islāmic sciences with excellence in the first degree of honor; major of Sciences of Ḥadīth from

the faculty of Ḥadīth and Islāmic studies 1426 A.H. (2006 A.H.).

- The charitable award of al-Madīnah; the award is for distinction and educational success and service; the year of 1427 A.H. (2007 C.E.).

<u>Among his Teachers</u>:

Shaykh ʿAbdul-Muḥsin al-Abbād al-Badr, whom he studied Ḥadīth.

<u>His works</u>:

- **<u>The books he verified</u>**:

1. *al-Imā Ilaa 'Atraaf Ahādīth Kitāb al-Muwatta* by Imām Abī al-'Abbas Ahmad ibn Ṭāhir a-Dani al-Andalusia (d. 532 A.H.). This was his thesis for the masters. This book is printed in five volumes by Al-Ma'arif publication in Riyāḍ.

2. al-*Mashāyakh* Al-*Baghdādīyah* by Abī Tahir Ahmad ibn Muḥammad ibn Ahmad al-Silfi al-Asbahānī (d. 576). This book was his doctoral thesis. He verified ten volumes of the book of overall 35 volumes.

3. The names of Mālik ibn ʾAnas's teachers by Shaykh Al-Muhaddith: Abī ʿAbdullāh Muḥammad ibn Ismā'il ibn ʿAbdur Raḥmān ibn Khalfūn al-Andalusī (d. 636 A.H.). One volume book printed by Adwaa al-Salaf publication 2004.

4. *Al-Ahādīth al Lati Khoulifa Feeha* Mālik ibn ʾAnas by al-Hāfidh Abī Alh-Hasan ad-Daraqutnī

Source of Biography:

http://www.ta3lime.com/showthread.php?t=41331

TRANSLITERATION TABLE

Consonants

ء	'	د	d	ض	ḍ	ك	k
ب	b	ذ	dh	ط	ṭ	ل	l
ت	t	ر	r	ظ	ẓ	م	m
ث	th	ز	z	ع	‘	ن	n
ج	j	س	s	غ	gh	هـ	h
ح	ḥ	ش	sh	ف	f	و	w
خ	kh	ص	ṣ	ق	q	ي	y

Vowels

Short	ـَ	a	ـِ	i	ـُ	u
Long	ـَا	ā	ـِي	ī	ـُو	ū

Dipthongs	ـَوْ	aw	ـَيْ	ay

Arabic Symbols & their meanings

حفظه الله	May Allāh preserve him
رَضِيَ ٱللَّهُ عَنْهُ	(i.e. a male companion of the Prophet Muḥammad)
سُبْحَانَهُ وَتَعَالَىٰ	Glorified & Exalted is Allāh
عَزَّ وَجَلَّ	(Allāh) the Mighty & Sublime
تَبَارَكَ وَتَعَالَىٰ	(Allāh) the Blessed & Exalted
جَلَّ وَعَلَا	(Allāh) the Sublime & Exalted
عَلَيْهِ ٱلصَّلَاةُ وَٱلسَّلَامُ	May Allāh send Blessings & Safety upon him (i.e. a Prophet or Messenger)
صَلَّى ٱللَّهُ عَلَيْهِ وَعَلَىٰ آلِهِ وَسَلَّمَ	May Allāh send Blessings & Safety upon him and his family (i.e. Du'ā sent when mentioning the Prophet Muḥammad)
رَحِمَهُ ٱللَّهُ	May Allāh have mercy upon him
رَضِيَ ٱللَّهُ عَنْهُمْ	May Allāh be pleased with them (i.e. Du'ā made for the Companions of the Prophet Muḥammad)
جَلَّ جَلَالُهُ	(Allāh) His Majesty is Exalted
رَضِيَ ٱللَّهُ عَنْهَا	رَضِيَ ٱللَّهُ عَنْهَا (i.e. a female companion of the Prophet Muḥammad)

INTRODUCTION

All praise is due to Allāh, who honored the children of ʾĀdam, both males and females, over a lot of His creation. He showed them the path of guidance and uprightness. He legislated a law for them in this world. He made no distinction between a male or a female regarding the obligation of obeying Him and following His path. He assigned obligations for both genders. He gave each their due rights; the male has his own rights as well as the female has her own rights. Humanity, throughout its entire history, has never witnessed a religion which cared so much about women in such perfection and devotion as Islām does.

Islām elevates the woman's status high enough to secure a unique position; she enjoys a respectable individuality and recognized rights and obligations. Islām hails her contributions and deems her as a major asset, who requires great care and attention. Islām considers her to be the man's partner since they both share a common creation. The Prophet (صَلَّىٱللَّهُعَلَيْهِوَسَلَّمَ) said,

إِنَّمَا النِّسَاءُ شَقَائِقُ الرِّجَالِ

"Indeed, women are partners of men."[1]

- As a child, Islām guarantees her right and urges to treat her kindly. Anas reported that the Prophet (صَلَّىٱللَّهُعَلَيْهِوَسَلَّمَ) said,

مَنْ عَالَ جَارِيَتَيْنِ حَتَّى تَبْلُغَا جَاءَ يَوْمَ الْقِيَامَةِ أَنَا وَ هُوَ كَهَاتَيْنِ.

"Whoever supports two girls till they reach maturity, he and I will come on the Day of Resurrection like this[2]."[3]

---

1 - Recorded by Abū Dāwud in *"as-Sunnan"*: (236), and it is authenticated by al-Albānī in *'as-Silsilah as-Saḥīḥah'*: (2863).

2 - **Translator's note:** The Prophet (صَلَّىٱللَّهُعَلَيْهِوَسَلَّمَ) joined his fingers expressing closeness between him and he who follows his instruction in this Ḥadīth.

3 - Recorded by Muslim: 2631.

- As a mother, Islām guarantees her right through urging to give her special treatment. Allāh says:

﴿ ۞ وَقَضَىٰ رَبُّكَ أَلَّا تَعْبُدُوٓا۟ إِلَّآ إِيَّاهُ وَبِٱلْوَٰلِدَيْنِ إِحْسَـٰنًا ۚ إِمَّا يَبْلُغَنَّ عِندَكَ ٱلْكِبَرَ أَحَدُهُمَآ أَوْ كِلَاهُمَا فَلَا تَقُل لَّهُمَآ أُفٍّ وَلَا تَنْهَرْهُمَا وَقُل لَّهُمَا قَوْلًا كَرِيمًا ﴿٢٣﴾ ﴾

"Your Lord has commanded that you worship none but Him and that you be good to your parents. If either of them or both of them reach old age with you, do not say to them a word of disrespect, nor scold them, but say to them kind words." [*Sūrah al-'Isrā'* 17:23]

- More importantly, Islām stresses emphatically on the right of the mother more than the father. Bahz ibn Ḥākim's grandfather said,

قُلْتُ : يَا رَسُولَ اللهِ ! مَنْ أَبَرُّ ؟ قَالَ : أُمَّكَ ثُمَّ أُمَّكَ ثُمَّ أُمَّكَ ثُمَّ أَبَاكَ ثُمَّ الْأَقْرَبَ فَالْأَقْرَبَ .

"I asked, 'Messenger of Allāh, to whom should I be dutiful?' 'Your mother, again your mother, again your mother, then your father, then your nearest relatives according to the order (of nearness).'"[4]

- As a wife, Islām guarantees her right. Her husband should observe her fundamental rights like kind treatment, gentleness, and generosity as ordained by Islām. The Prophet (صَلَّى ٱللَّٰهُ عَلَيْهِ وَسَلَّمَ) instructed (husbands),

أَلَا وَاسْتَوْصُوا بِالنِّسَاءِ خَيْرًا ؛ فَإِنَّهُنَّ عَوَانٍ عِنْدَكُمْ .

"Treat women kindly, as they are under your command."[5]

4 - Recorded by Abū Dāwud in *'al-Sunnan'*: (5139) and it was authenticated by al-Albānī in *'Irwā' al-Ghalīl*: (837).
5 - Recorded by al-Tirmidhī: (1163).

- Islām guarantees her right as a sister and both paternal and maternal aunts. The Prophet (صَلَّى ٱللَّهُ عَلَيْهِ وَسَلَّمَ) said,

الْخَالَةُ بِمَنْزِلَةِ الأُمِّ

"The maternal aunt is at the same status as the mother."[6]

These are some of the women's rights instructed by Islām. Evidently, the status of women (in Islām) is significantly more important than what is imagined by those who call for her liberty, as they claim. Women in Islām are as accountable for observing the obligations of Islām as men are as well as the consequential reward or punishment.

Allāh says,

---

[6] - Recorded by al-Bukhārī: (2699).

﴿ وَمَن يَعْمَلْ مِنَ ٱلصَّٰلِحَٰتِ مِن ذَكَرٍ أَوْ أُنثَىٰ وَهُوَ مُؤْمِنٌ فَأُو۟لَٰٓئِكَ يَدْخُلُونَ ٱلْجَنَّةَ وَلَا يُظْلَمُونَ نَقِيرًا ﴿١٢٤﴾ ﴾

"And whoever does righteous deeds, whether male or female, while being a believer - those will enter Paradise and will not be wronged, [even as much as] the speck of a date seed." [*Sūrah an-Nisā'* 4:124]

And,

﴿ مَنْ عَمِلَ صَٰلِحًا مِّن ذَكَرٍ أَوْ أُنثَىٰ وَهُوَ مُؤْمِنٌ فَلَنُحْيِيَنَّهُۥ حَيَوٰةً طَيِّبَةً ۖ وَلَنَجْزِيَنَّهُمْ أَجْرَهُم بِأَحْسَنِ مَا كَانُوا۟ يَعْمَلُونَ ﴿٩٧﴾ ﴾

"Whoever does righteousness, whether male or female, while he is a believer - We will surely cause him to live a good life, and We will surely give them their reward [in the Hereafter]

according to the best of what they used to do." [*Sūrah an-Naḥl* 16:97]

Therefore, women are as entrusted with the trust of Islām as men. This includes applying its instructions and promoting its ideals and morals. It is impossible to set her aside from the Muslim society because, unequivocally, she has an evident and apparent impact on it. Furthermore, since she has rights and obligations as proven earlier, she is an integral part of this society.

She is trustworthy and eminently qualified as a consultant. She was even, at the beginning of Islām, a teacher for the generations; educating, teaching, and guiding them to the clear and straight path by virtue of what Allāh gifted her with influencing the hearts of both males and females. For this particular reason, her role was limited to instructing others against diverting from the truth and treading means of misguidance. She is included as well as required to apply the Prophet's saying,

الدِّينُ النَّصِيحَةُ، قُلْنَا : لِمَنْ ؟ قَالَ : لله وَ لِكِتَابِهِ وَ لِرَسُولِهِ وَ لِأَئِمَّةِ الْمُسْلِمِينَ وَ عَامَّتِهِمْ.

"The Dīn (religion) is naṣīḥah (advice, sincerity)," We said, "To whom?" He (صَلَّى ٱللَّهُ عَلَيْهِ وَسَلَّمَ) said, "To Allāh, His Book, His Messenger, and to the leaders of the Muslims and their common folk."[7]

A woman is an advisor, a guide, and an educator. Her advice for others contributes to making life more settling and full of tranquility and happiness; because she can address souls by guiding them to what will reform and lead them to success out of love for whoever is advised and out of desire for the good and reform of their souls; since she is gifted with nice speech, faithful intentions, intense and deep emotions that substantially lead the minds of sinners to safety and success.

This book points out the position of the woman in the field of Dʿawah in general and her position in giving advice in particular. This very woman is an integral part

---

7 - Recorded in Ṣaḥīḥ Muslim: (55).

of the society; she is a daughter, a sister, a wife, and a mother. She could be at her house or her parent's house; she could be outside her house in the company of her friends and colleagues. At all of these places, she hears and sees whoever is around her whether it is good or bad. Notably, our pure religion commands the woman the same as the man to actively change evil once sighting it.

Allāh says,

﴿ وَٱلۡمُؤۡمِنُونَ وَٱلۡمُؤۡمِنَٰتُ بَعۡضُهُمۡ أَوۡلِيَآءُ بَعۡضٖۚ يَأۡمُرُونَ
بِٱلۡمَعۡرُوفِ وَيَنۡهَوۡنَ عَنِ ٱلۡمُنكَرِ وَيُقِيمُونَ ٱلصَّلَوٰةَ وَيُؤۡتُونَ
ٱلزَّكَوٰةَ وَيُطِيعُونَ ٱللَّهَ وَرَسُولَهُۥٓۚ أُوْلَٰٓئِكَ سَيَرۡحَمُهُمُ ٱللَّهُۗ
إِنَّ ٱللَّهَ عَزِيزٌ حَكِيمٞ ٧١ ﴾

"The believers, men, and women, are ʾAwliyāʾ (helpers, supporters, friends, protectors) of one another, they enjoin (on the people) al-Maʿrūf (i.e. Islāmic Monotheism and all that Islām orders one to do), and forbid (people) from al-Munkar (i.e.

polytheism and disbelief of all kinds, and all that Islām has forbidden); they perform as-Salāt and give the Zakāt, and obey Allāh and His Messenger. Allāh will have His Mercy on them. Surely Allāh is All-Mighty, All-Wise." [*Sūrah at-Tawbah* 9:71]

The Prophet (صَلَّى ٱللَّهُ عَلَيْهِ وَسَلَّمَ) said,

مَنْ رَأَى مِنْكُمْ مُنْكَرًا فَلْيُغَيِّرْهُ بِيَدِهِ، فَإِنْ لَمْ يَسْتَطِعْ فَبِلِسَانِهِ، فَإِنْ لَمْ يَسْتَطِعْ فَبِقَلْبِهِ، وَ ذَلِكَ أَضْعَفُ الْإِيمَانِ.

"Whosoever of you sees an evil, let him change it with his hand; and if he is not able to do so, then [let him change it] with his tongue; and if he is not able to do so, then with his heart — and that is the weakest of faith."[8]

This instruction is general and addresses both men and women on an equal footing. The woman's part in

8 -Recorded by Muslim: (49).

changing evil is to be observed consistently with the legislative regulations, and giving advice is a part of it. She is expected to advise her fellow women in accordance to what she is blessed with of knowledge and wisdom. There are examples from the best centuries where the woman gave advice at her house and outside it. Thus, I have seen it fit to divide this book into two sections; each section is comprised of several chapters. At the end of the book, I gave some recommendations for women pertaining giving advice. Indeed, Allāh is the One, who leads to all that is good.

SECTION 1: ADVISING INSIDE THE HOUSE AND ITS DESCRIPTION

Introduction

Settling in the house is an innate nature within the woman which Allāh created her with. A considerate observation in the woman's psychology would reveal that she loves to stay in the house for entertainment and amusement. As opposed to the male who may feel controlled by staying in the house. This natural disposition in the woman has been made clearer in Allāh's command for the women to stay home.

Allāh says,

﴿ وَقَرْنَ فِي بُيُوتِكُنَّ ﴾

"And stay in your houses." [*Sūrah al-Ahzāb* 32:33]

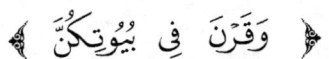

SECTION 1: ADVISING INSIDE THE HOUSE AND ITS DESCRIPTION

In addition, Allāh entrusted the woman with some obligations and tasks inside the house. A woman inside the house is, for the most part, a mother, a daughter, a sister or a wife. Each one has certain roles and obligations inside the house where each lives at. The woman's role in Islām is not only limited to her being a mother, but rather she has a job as a mother, a sister, a daughter, and a wife. She takes care of her husband's affairs, an educator and is in charge of her children; in a nutshell, she is the trusted companion and the loyal friend. One of those tasks is advising the house residents since she is a part and an active member of it.

The following chapters tackle the manner with which the woman can offer her advice to the habitants of her home.

CHAPTER 1: THE MOTHER'S ROLE IN ADVISING HER CHILDREN

Motherhood is one of the greatest and prestigious qualities of women. Allāh ordained various rulings that stem from motherhood; rulings related to pregnancy, breastfeeding, kindness, mercy, and other matters of this sort that flow out of her heart. Not to mention her overwhelming emotions towards her children; she is the one who carries, breastfeed, educate them, and stay sleepless for the sake of their comfort. Accordingly, Allāh rewarded her with making paradise under her feet.

It is narrated from Muʿāwiyah bin Jāhimah as-Salamī, who came to the Prophet (ﷺ) and said:

يَا رَسُولَ اللهِ ! أَرَدْتُ أَنْ أَغْزُوَ وَ قَدْ جِئْتُ أَسْتَشِيرُكَ ، فَقَالَ : هَلْ لَكَ مِنْ أُمٍّ ؟ ، قَالَ : نَعَمْ ! قَالَ : فَالْزَمْهَا فَإِنَّ الْجَنَّةَ تَحْتَ رِجْلَيْهَا .

> **"O Messenger of Allāh! I want to go out and fight (in Jihād), and I have come to ask your advice." He said: "Do you have a mother?" He said: "Yes." He said: "Then stay with her, for Paradise is beneath her feet."**[9]

The mother in her house is responsible for her children because she outstays the father in the house, who is mostly preoccupied with livelihood outside the house. This ought to make her in close contact with the children more than the father especially during their early years. Therefore, she is obliged to educate and advise them in addition to reminding them to observe their obligations towards their Lord and their society. So, her influence on the hearts of her children is obviously undeniable. Evidently, the Prophet (صَلَّى ٱللَّهُ عَلَيْهِ وَسَلَّمَ) attributed the shift in the children's nature to both of their parents and not only to the father. The Prophet (صَلَّى ٱللَّهُ عَلَيْهِ وَسَلَّمَ) said,

---

[9] - Recorded by al-Nasā'ī in as-Sunnan: (3104), and it was rendered Ḥasan (sound) by al-Albānī in 'Irwā' al-Ghalīl: (5/21).

مَا مِنْ مَوْلُودٍ إِلَّا يُولَدُ عَلَى الْفِطْرَةِ ، فَأَبَوَاهُ يُهَوِّدَانِهِ ، أَوْ يُنَصِّرَانِهِ ، أَوْ يُمَجِّسَانِهِ ، كَمَا تُنْتِجُ الْبَهِيمَةُ بَهِيمَةً جَمْعَاءَ ، هَلْ تَحُسُّونَ فِيهَا مِنْ جَدْعَاءَ ؟

"There is none born but is created to his true nature (Islām). It is his parents who make him a Jew or a Christian or a Magian quite as beasts produce their young with their limbs perfect. Do you see anything deficient in them?"[10]

The mother's primary focus should center on teaching her children the sound ʿAqīdah (Creed) and the Oneness of the Creator. The next step is teaching them about the best of mankind including following and loving him; plus, the other religion-related matters that must be known.

The early Salafī women were strongly keen to advise their children. Ḥudhayfah (رَضِيَ اللَّهُ عَنْهُ) narrated,

10 - Recorded by a-Bukhārī: (1359) and Muslim: (2658).

سَأَلَتْنِي أُمِّي مَتَى عَهْدُكَ ؟ تَعْنِي بِالنَّبِيِّ صَلَّى اللهُ عَلَيْهِ وَ سَلَّمَ ، فَقُلْتُ : مَا لِي بِهِ عَهْدٌ مُنْذُ كَذَا وَ كَذَا ، فَنَالَتْ مِنِّي ، فَقُلْتُ لَهَا : دَعِينِي آتِي النَّبِيَّ صَلَّى اللهُ وَ عَلَيْهِ وَ سَلَّمَ فَأُصَلِّي مَعَهُ الْمَغْرِبَ وَ أَسْأَلُهُ أَنْ يَسْتَغْفِرَ لِي وَ لَكِ ، فَأَتَيْتُ النَّبِيَّ صَلَّى اللهُ عَلَيْهِ وَ سَلَّمَ فَصَلَّيْتُ مَعَهُ الْمَغْرِبَ ، فَصَلَّى حَتَّى صَلَّى الْعِشَاءَ ، ثُمَّ انْفَتَلَ فَتَبِعْتُهُ ، فَسَمِعَ صَوْتِي فَقَالَ : مَنْ هَذَا ؛ حُذَيْفَةُ ؟ ، قُلْتُ : نَعَمْ ؛ قَالَ : مَا حَاجَتُكَ غَفَرَ اللهُ لَكَ وَ لِأُمِّكَ ؟ ، قَالَ : إِنَّ هَذَا مَلَكٌ لَمْ يَنْزِلِ الْأَرْضَ قَطُّ قَبْلَ هَذِهِ اللَّيْلَةِ ، اسْتَأْذَنَ رَبَّهُ أَنْ يُسَلِّمَ عَلَيَّ وَ يُبَشِّرَنِي بِأَنْ فَاطِمَةَ سَيِّدَةُ نِسَاءِ أَهْلِ الْجَنَّةِ ، وَ أَنَّ الْحَسَنَ وَ الْحُسَيْنَ سَيِّدَا شَبَابِ أَهْلِ الْجَنَّةِ .

"My mother asked me: 'When is your planned time - meaning with the Prophet (صَلَّى اللَّهُ عَلَيْهِ وَسَلَّمَ)?' So I said: 'I have not had a planned time to see him since such and such time.' She rebuked me, so I said to her: 'Let me go to the Prophet (صَلَّى اللَّهُ عَلَيْهِ وَسَلَّمَ) so that I may perform Maghrib (prayer) with him, and ask him to seek forgiveness for you and I.' So I came to the Prophet (صَلَّى اللَّهُ عَلَيْهِ وَسَلَّمَ), and I prayed Maghrib with him, and then he prayed until he prayed al-ʿIshāʾ.

Then he turned, and I followed him, and he heard my voice, and said: 'Who is this? Ḥudhayfah?' I said: 'Yes.' He said: "What is your need, may Allāh forgive you and your mother?' He said: 'Indeed, this is an angel that never descended to the earth ever before tonight. He sought permission from his Lord to greet me with peace and to give me the glad tidings that Fatimah is the chief of the women in Paradise, and that al-Ḥasan and al-

Ḥusayn are the chiefs of the youths of the people of Paradise.'" [11]

The mother of Ḥudhayfah (رَضِيَٱللَّهُعَنْهَا) advised her son to visit the Prophet every now and then so that his faith would increase as well as his love (for the Prophet). However, she scolded him after she found out he has not visited him for quite some time. This would make him bring his attention to something he may consider unworthy while, in fact, it is worthwhile. This is an example of a mother advising her son, and this is the way it should be.

Furthermore, the mother should always remind her children to observe acts of worship and obedience. The Prophet (صَلَّىٱللَّهُعَلَيْهِوَسَلَّمَ) ordered the parents to command their children to perform prayer. He said,

---

[11] - Recorded by al-Tirmidhī in al-Jāmi': (3781) and Ahmad in 'al-Musnad': (38/353).

مُرُوا أَوْلَادَكُمْ بِالصَّلَاةِ وَ هُمْ أَبْنَاءُ سَبْعِ سِنِينَ ، وَاضْرِبُوهُمْ عَلَيْهَا وَ هُمْ أَبْنَاءُ عَشْرٍ ، وَ فَرِّقُوا بَيْنَهُمْ فِي الْمَضَاجِعِ .

"Command your children to perform Ṣalāh (prayer) when they are seven years old, and beat them for (not offering) it when they are ten, and do not let (boys and girls) sleep together."[12]

The mother should be persistent in not only advising her children to commit themselves to embody moral principles and noble ideals but also educating them to be as such; because she is considered the teacher of those generations. They learn and take example of being straight from her.

'Anas narrated,

12 - Recorded by Abū Dāwud in 'al-Sunan': (496) and Ahmad in 'al-Musnad': (11/369).

قَدِمَ النَّبِيُّ الْمَدِينَةَ وَ أَنَا ابْنُ تِسْعِ سِنِينَ ، فَانْطَلَقَتْ بِي أُمِّي أُمُّ سُلَيْمٍ إِلَى نَبِيِّ اللهِ صَلَّى اللهُ عَلَيْهِ وَ سَلَّمَ ، فَقَالَتْ : يَا رَسُولَ اللهِ ! هَذَا ابْنِي اسْتَخْدِمْهُ ، فَخَدَمْتُ النَّبِيَّ صَلَّى اللهُ عَلَيْهِ تِسْعَ سِنِينَ ، فَمَا قَالَ لِي لِشَيْءٍ فَعَلْتُهُ : لِمَا فَعَلْتَ كَذَا وَ كَذَا ، وَ مَا قَالَ لِي لِشَيْءٍ لَمْ أَفْعَلْهُ : أَ لَا فَعَلْتَ كَذَا وَ كَذَا . وَ أَتَانِي ذَاتَ يَوْمٍ وَ أَنَا أَلْعَبُ مَعَ الْغِلْمَانِ – أَوْ قَالَ : مَعَ الصِّبْيَانِ – فَسَلَّمَ عَلَيْنَا ، ثُمَّ دَعَانِي فَأَرْسَلَنِي فِي حَاجَةٍ ، فَلَمَّا رَجَعْتُ قَالَ : لَا تُخْبِرْ أَحَدًا ، فَاحْتُبِسْتُ عَلَى أُمِّي ، فَلَمَّا أَتَيْتُهَا قَالَتْ : يَا بُنَيَّ ، مَا حبسك ؟ قُلْتُ : أَرْسَلَنِي رَسُولَ اللهِ صَلَّى اللهُ عَلَيْهِ وَ سَلَّمَ فِي حَاجَةٍ لَهُ ، قَالَتْ : وَ مَا هِيَ ؟ قُلْتُ : إِنَّهُ قَالَ : لَا تُخْبِرَنَّ بِهَا

أَحَدًا ؛ قَالَتْ : أَي بُنَيَّ ، فَاكْتُمْ عَلَى رَسُولِ اللهِ صَلَّى اللهُ عَلَيْهِ وَ سَلَّمَ سِرَّهُ .

"The Prophet (ﷺ) arrived at Madīnah when I was nine years old. My mother, 'Umm Sulaym, took me and headed straight to the Prophet of Allāh. She said, "O Messenger of Allāh, here is my son! Take him as your servant.' 'Anas continued, 'I served the Prophet for nine years; he never asked me about a thing which I had done why I did that or about a thing I had left as to why I had not done that."

One day, the Prophet (ﷺ) came while I was playing with my playmates. He greeted us and then called me and sent me on an errand. After I had come back, he said, "Do not tell anyone!" This detained me from going home for some time. So when I arrived home, my mother asked me, 'What took you so long?" I said, 'The Prophet sent me on an errand?' She asked, 'what was it?' I told her, 'the Prophet (ﷺ) told me not to tell anyone.'

> **She said, 'Ok, do not divulge the secret of Allāh's Messenger."**[13]

The mother of ʾAnas advised him not to divulge the secret of Allāh's Messenger. She advised him to maintain such high ideal. She would not fall for the Shayṭān's (trap) of being curious to know the secret. Shaykh Muḥammad ibn Ṣālih al-ʿUthaymīn noted some benefits from this Ḥadīth. He said,

> **"ʾUmm Sulaym educated her son well when she advised him to keep the secret of Allāh's Messenger. The reason for her advice, despite he had not told her or anybody else, is being encouraging and supportive, since he refused to tell her in the first place because it is the secret of Allāh's Messenger. It is as if she said, 'I approve your action so commit to it."**[14]

Likewise, ʾUmm ad-Dardāʾ, a Tabīʿ woman (successor), was very keen to educate children and advise them to

---

[13] - Recorded by Muslim: (2482) and Ahmad in 'al-Musnad': (20/182). The above wording is Ahmad's.

[14] - The explanation of Riyāḍ as-Ṣālihīn: chapter: keeping the secret: (4/43).

adhere to good morals. ʿAbdul-Rabī ibn Sulaymān ibn ʿUmayr narrated,

كَانَتْ أُمُّ الدَّرْدَاءِ تَكْتُبُ لِي فِي لَوْحِي فِيمَا تعلّمني مِنَ الْحِكْمَةِ: تَعَلَّمُوا الْحِكْمَةَ صِغَارًا تَعْمَلُوا بِهَا كِبَارًا، وَ إِنَّ كُلَّ زَارِعٍ حَاصِدٌ، مَا زَرَعَ مِنْ خَيْرٍ أَوْ شَرٍّ.

"ʾUmm ad-Dardāʾ used to write in my notebook words of wisdom, where she said, 'Learn wisdom during your youth so that you would apply it when you grow up; every planter, whether good or bad, shall eventually harvest.'[15]

ʿUthmān ibn Hayan narrated,

أَكَلْنَا مَعَ أُمِّ الدَّرْدَاءِ طَعَامًا فَأَغْفَلْنَا: الْحَمْدُ للهِ، فَقَالَتْ: يَا بُنَيَّ! لَا تَدَعُوا أَنْ تُؤَدمُوا طَعَامَكُمْ بِذِكْرِ اللهِ؛ أَكْلٌ وَ حَمْدٌ خَيْرٌ مِنْ أَكْلٍ وَ صَمْتٍ.

15 - Taḥdhīb al-Kamāl: (35/355).

"We ate with ʾUmm ad-Dardāʾ once, but we forgot to say: al-Ḥamdulillah. She said, 'Son! Do not miss out on the blessing your food with Allāh's remembrance; eating followed by expressing gratitude to Allāh is better than eating with silence."[16]

Furthermore, al-ʿAliyah Bint Shurayk, the mother of Imām Mālik ibn ʾAnas, used to advise her son to learn manners, self-composure, and forbearance before learning knowledge.

Muṭarrif narrated that Mālik said:

قُلْتُ لِأُمِّي : أَذْهَبُ فَأَكْتُبُ الْعِلْمَ ؟ فَقَالَتْ : تَعَالَ فَالْبَسْ ثِيَابَ الْعِلْمِ ، فَأَلْبَسَتْنِي ثِيَابًا مُشَمَّرَةً وَ وَضَعَتْ الطَّوِيلَةَ عَلَى رَأْسِي وَ عَمَّمَتْنِي فَوْقَهَا ، ثُمَّ قَالَتْ : اِذْهَبْ فَاكْتُبِ الْآنَ . وَ قَالَ رَحِمَهُ اللهُ : ((كَانَتْ

16 - Taḥdhīb al-Kamāl: (35/357).

أُمِّي تُعَمِّمُنِي وَ تَقُولُ لِي : اِذْهَبْ إِلَى رَبِيعَةَ فَتَعَلَّمْ مِنْ أَدَبِهِ قَبْلَ عِلْمِهِ)).

"I asked my mother to go and learn knowledge. She told him, 'Come! Put on the clothes of knowledge. She dressed me and put a turban on my head. Then she said, 'Go and learn now.' He also said, 'My mother used to put a turban on my head and tell me: go to Rabīʿah (a famous scholar) and learn his manners before his knowledge."[17]

These are few examples that illustrate mothers giving advice to their children. So, it is more adequate for the mother to follow their example.

---

[17] - Tartīb al-Madārik by al-Qāḍī ʿIyāḍ: (1/130).

CHAPTER 2: THE DAUGHTER'S ROLE IN ADVISING HER PARENTS

Allāh may bless the children to be committed to His religion but not their parents. There are several instances of such matter in our contemporary time. So, instead of the parents being the role model for the daughter, we find that Allāh blessed the daughter with the love of a committed religious life; however, she faces many obstacles on her way. Of those obstacles, parents stand as the most difficult particularly in some of the Westernized communities that were influenced by the Western civilization.

There are many daughters who complain from the mistreatment of their parents because they wore the legal Hijab or committed to obeying and worshipping Allāh; which obviously drove her away from many prohibitions like intermingling with men, music, prohibited (kind) of traveling, impermissible gatherings, and so on. Some of them inquire about the (appropriate) way of dealing with their parents; should they remain steadfast on worship and withstand the collateral harm or should they take a stand against that mistreatment?

Undoubtedly, the daughter is obliged to obey her parents as long as it does not involve disobeying Allāh. She is obliged to please them and provide them with physical and mental comfort. Most importantly, their benefit, education, bringing them close to Allāh and driving them away from what displeases Him should be on her priority list. This is the best gift a daughter could ever present her parents with. The ultimate expression of obedience to them is that she can be the reason they enter Paradise and be saved from the hellfire.

This will be achievable only when she consistently offers advice for them in a subtle way and by maintaining good behavior; because if the human being is distant from Allāh, he likely does not listen to the advice of who is beneath him, let alone listen to it from whom he was a means for their existence (i.e. the daughter). The daughter must consider this situation very carefully and maintain patience throughout it; for indeed, this is the ultimate expression of obedience to parents. She should seek to advise them from time to time in matters where they are distant from being right; like falling into acts of disbelief as in supplicating to other than Allāh, grave worshipping, visiting magicians, and fortunetellers, besides other forms of Shirk that oppose the pure Tawhīd.

The daughter should also explain the pillars of Islām and call them to comply with Allāh's commands through performing prayer, paying Zakāt, and the rest of obligations; in addition to abandoning the prohibitions, wrongdoings, and immorality. She must maintain wisdom and friendliness as well as kindness and believing that she will always fall short in repaying their debt even if they are disbelievers or disobedient.

'Asmā' Bint Abī Bakr (رَضِيَ اللَّهُ عَنْهَا) said,

قَدِمَتْ عَلَيَّ أُمِّي وَ هِيَ مُشْرِكَةٌ فِي عَهْدِ رَسُولِ الله صَلَّى اللهُ عَلَيْهِ وَ سَلَّمَ ، فَاسْتَفْتَيتُ رَسُولَ الله صَلَّى اللهُ عَلَيْهِ وَ سَلَّمَ ، قُلْتُ : إِنَّ أُمِّي قَدِمَتْ وَ هِيَ رَاغِبَةٌ ، أَ فَأَصِلُ أُمِّي ؟ قَالَ : نَعَمْ صِلِي أُمَّكِ .

"My mother came to me while she was still a polytheist, so I asked the Messenger of Allāh (صَلَّىٱللَّهُعَلَيْهِوَسَلَّمَ), "My mother, who disbelieves in Islām, has come to visit me. Shall I maintain relations with her?" He (صَلَّىٱللَّهُعَلَيْهِوَسَلَّمَ) replied, "Yes, maintain relations with your mother."[18]

Moreover, there are lots of benefits derived from the story of Abū Hurayrah's mother conversion to Islām. It represents the finest way for the daughter to follow in guiding her parents and enduring the collateral harm.

Abū Hurayrah narrated,

كُنْتُ أَدْعُو أُمِّي إِلَى الإِسْلَامِ وَ هِيَ مُشْرِكَةٌ، فَدَعَوْتُهَا يَوْمًا فَأَسْمَعَتْنِي فِي رَسُولِ اللهِ صَلَّى اللهُ عَلَيْهِ وَ سَلَّمَ مَا أَكْرَهُ، فَأَتَيْتُ رَسُولَ اللهِ وَ أَنَا أَبْكِي، قُلْتُ: يَا رَسُولَ اللهِ! إِنِّي كُنْتُ أَدْعُو أُمِّي إِلَى الإِسْلَامِ فَتَأْبَى عَلَيَّ، فَدَعَوْتُهَا الْيَوْمَ فَأَسْمَعَتْنِي فِيكَ مَا أَكْرَهُ، فَادْعُ اللهَ أَنْ

---

18 - Recorded by al-Bukhārī: (2620) and Muslim: (1003).

يَـهْـدِيَ أُمَّ هُـرَيْـرَةَ ، فَـقَـالَ رَسُـولُ اللهِ صَـلَّـى اللهُ عَـلَـيْـهِ وَ سَـلَّـمَ

: الـلَّـهُـمَّ اهْـدِ أُمَّ أَبِـي هُـرَيْـرَةَ ، فَـخَـرَجْـتُ مُـسْـتَـبْـشِـرًا بِـدَعْـوَةِ

نَـبِـيِّ اللهِ صَـلَّـى اللهُ عَـلَـيْـهِ وَ سَـلَّـمَ ، فَـلَـمَّـا جِـئْـتُ فَـصُـرْتُ

إِلَـى الْـبَـابِ ، فَـإِذَا هُـوَ مُـجَـافٍ ، فَـسَـمِـعَـتْ أُمِّـي خَـشِـفَ

قَـدَمَـيَّ ، فَـقَـالَـتْ : مَـكَـانَـكَ يَـا أَبَـا هُـرَيْـرَةَ ، وَ سَـمِـعْـتُ

خَـضْـخَـضَـةَ الْـمَـاءِ ، قَـالَ : فَـاغْـتَـسَـلَـتْ وَ لَـبِـسَـتْ دِرعَـهَـا

وَ عَـجِـلَـتْ عَـنْ خِـمَـارِهَـا فَـفَـتِـحَـتِ الْـبَـابَ ، ثُـمَّ قَـالَـتْ :

يَـا أَبَـا هُـرَيْـرَةَ ! أَشْـهَـدُ أَنْ لَا إِلَـهَ إِلَّا اللهُ وَ أَشْـهَـدُ أَنَّ

مُـحَـمَّـدًا عَـبْـدُهُ وَ رَسُـولُـهُ . قَـالَ : فَـرَجِـعْـتُ إِلَـى رَسُـولِ اللهِ

صَـلَّـى اللهُ عَـلَـيْـهِ وَ سَـلَّـمَ فَـأَتَـيْـتُـهُ وَ أَنَـا أَبْـكِـي مِـنَ الْـفَـرِحِ

، قَـالَ : قُـلْـتُ : يَـا رَسُـولَ اللهِ ! أَبْـشِـرْ ، قَـدِ اسْـتَـجَـابَ اللهُ

دَعْـوَتَـكَ ، وَ هَـدَى أُمَّ أَبِـي هُـرَيْـرَةَ ، فَـحَـمِـدَ اللهَ وَ أَثْـنَـى

عَـلَـيْـهِ وَ قَـالَ خَـيْـرًا ، قَـالَ : قُـلْـتُ : يَـا رَسُـولَ اللهِ ! ادْعُ اللهَ

أَنْ يُحَبِّبَنِي أَنَا وَ أُمِّي إِلَى عِبَادِهِ الْمُؤْمِنِينَ ، وَ يُحَبِّبَهُمْ إِلَيْنَا ، قَالَ : فَقَالَ رَسُولَ اللهِ صَلَّى اللهُ عَلَيْهِ وَ سَلَّمَ : اللَّهُمَّ حَبِّبْ عُبَيْدَكَ هَذَا - يَعْنِي أَبَا هُرَيْرَة - وَ أُمَّهُ إِلَى عِبَادِكَ الْمُؤْمِنِينَ ، وَ حَبِّبْ إِلَيْهِمُ الْمُؤْمِنِينَ ، فَمَا خُلق يَسْمَعُ بِي وَ لَا يَرَانِي إِلَّا أَحَبَّنِي

.

"I invited my mother, who was a polytheist, to Islām. I invited her one day, and she said to me something about Allāh's Messenger (ﷺ) which I hated. I went to Allāh's Messenger (ﷺ) weeping and said: Allāh's Messenger, I invited my mother to Islām, but she did not accept (my invitation). I invited her today, but she said to me something ill about you which I did not like. (Kindly) Supplicate to Allāh that He may set the mother of Abū Hurayrah right. Thereupon Allāh's Messenger (ﷺ) said: O Allāh, set the mother of Abū Hurayrah on the right path. I

left quite pleased with the supplication of Allāh's Messenger (صَلَّىٰ ٱللَّهُ عَلَيْهِ وَسَلَّمَ) and when I came near the door it was closed from within. My mother heard the noise of my footsteps, and she said: Abū Hurayrah, just wait. Moreover, I heard the noise of falling of water. She took a bath and put on her clothes and quickly covered her head with a headdress and opened the door and then said: Abū Hurayrah, I bear witness that there is none has the right to be worshiped in truth except Allāh, and that Muḥammad is His servant and His Messenger.'

He (Abū Hurayrah) said: I went back to Allāh's Messenger (صَلَّىٰ ٱللَّهُ عَلَيْهِ وَسَلَّمَ) and (this time) I was shedding tears of joy. I said: Allāh's Messenger, be happy, for Allāh has responded to your supplication, and He has set on the right path the mother of Abū Hurayrah. He (the Prophet) praised Allāh, and extolled Him and uttered good words. I said: Allāh's Messenger, supplicate to Allāh so that He may instill love of mine and that of my mother too in the believing servants and let our hearts be filled with their love, whereupon

Allāh's Messenger (صَلَّى ٱللَّهُ عَلَيْهِ وَسَلَّمَ) said: 'O Allāh, let there be love of these servants of yours, i.e. Abu Hurayrah and his mother, in the hearts of the believing servants and let their hearts be filled with the love of the believing servants.' (Abū Hurayrah said: This prayer) was so well granted by Allāh that no believer was ever born who heard of me and who saw me but did not love me."[19]

This example teaches the daughter to be very zealous in guiding her parents towards the straight path, supplicating for them, and offering them advice; and this indeed is the best a dutiful daughter could do for her parents. Whenever she notices some kind of slackness or ignorance from her parents, it should be her who rectifies them and guides them back to the straight path; and everybody will be a winner. The following narration includes an example of how a daughter should advise her parents. It also shows how the daughter clarified for her parents the proper belief and action that should be taken in response to the command and choice of the Messenger of Allāh (صَلَّى ٱللَّهُ عَلَيْهِ وَسَلَّمَ) even if this course of

19 - Recorded by Muslim: (2491).

action would superficially make them feel inconvenient as well as their daughter; however, the best choice is what is chosen by the Messenger (ﷺ). This reflects a perfection in one's faith and total compliance to the Messenger.

Abū Barzah al-Aslamī said:

أَنَّ جُلَيْبِيبًا كَانَ امْرَأً يَدْخُلُ عَلَى النِّسَاءِ، يَمُرُّ بِهِنَّ وَ يُلَاعِبُهُنَّ ، فَقُلْتُ لِامْرَأَتِي : لَا يَدْخُلُنَّ عَلَيْكُمْ جُلَيْبِيبٌ ؛ فَإِنَّهُ إِنْ دَخَلَ عَلَيْكُمْ لَأَفْعَلَنَّ وَ لَأَفْعَلَنَّ . قَالَ : وَ كَانَتِ الْأَنْصَارُ إِذَا كَانَ لِأَحَدِهِمْ أَيِّمٌ لَمْ يُزَوِّجْهَا حَتَّى يَعْلَمَ هَلْ لِلنَّبِيِّ صَلَّى اللهُ عَلَيْهِ وَ سَلَّمَ فِيهَا حَاجَةٌ أَمْ لَا ، فَقَالَ رَسُولُ اللهِ صَلَّى اللهُ عَلَيْهِ وَ سَلَّمَ لِرَجُلٍ مِنَ الْأَنْصَارِ : زَوِّجْنِي ابْنَتَكَ ، فَقَالَ : نَعَمْ ؛ وَ كَرَامَةً يَا رَسُولَ اللهِ ! وَ نُعْمَ عَيْنِي ، قَالَ : إِنِّي لَسْتُ أُرِيدُهَا لِنَفْسِي . قَالَ : فَلِمَنْ يَا رَسُولَ

اللهِ ؟ قَالَ : لِجُلَيْبِيب . قَالَ : فَقَالَ : يَا رَسُولَ اللهِ ! أُشَاوِرُ أُمَّهَا ، فَأَتَى أُمَّهَا فَقَالَ : رَسُولُ اللهِ صَلَّى اللهُ عَلَيْهِ وَ سَلَّمَ يَخْطُبُ ابْنَتَكَ ؛ فَقَالَتْ : نَعَمْ ، وَ نُعْمَةُ عَيْنِي ! فَقَالَ : إِنَّهُ لَيْسَ يَخْطُبُهَا لِنَفْسِهِ ، إِنَّمَا يَخْطُبُهَا لِجُلَيْبِيب . فَقَالَتْ : أَ جُلَيْبِيبٌ إِنِيهِ ؟ أَ جُلَيْبِيبٌ إِنِيهِ ؟ أَ جُلَيْبِيبٌ إِنِيهِ ؟ لَا ، لَعمْر اللهِ لَا نُزَوِّجُهُ . فَلَمَّا أَرَادَ أَنْ يَقُومَ لِيَأْتِيَ رَسُولَ اللهِ صَلَّى اللهُ عَلَيْهِ وَ سَلَّمَ فَيُخْبِرُهُ بِمَا قَالَتْ أُمُّهَا ، قَالَتِ الْجَارِيَةُ : مَنْ خَطِبَنِي إِلَيْكُمْ ؟ فَأَخْبَرَتْهَا أُمُّهَا فَقَالَتْ : أَ تَرُدُّونَ عَلَى رَسُولِ اللهِ صَلَّى اللهُ عَلَيْهِ وَ سَلَّمَ أَمْرَهُ ؟ ادْفَعُونِي ؛ فَإِنَّهُ لَمْ يُضَيِّعْنِي . فَانْطَلَقَ أَبُوهَا إِلَى رَسُولِ اللهِ صَلَّى اللهُ عَلَيْهِ فَأَخْبَرَهُ فَقَالَ : شَأْنَكَ بِهَا ، فَزَوَّجَهَا جُلَيْبِيبًا . قَالَ : فَخَرَجَ رَسُولُ اللهِ صَلَّى اللهُ عَلَيْهِ وَ

سَلَّمَ فِي غَزْوَةٍ لَهُ ، قَالَ : فَلَمَّا أَفَاءَ اللهُ عَلَيْهِ قَالَ لِأَصْحَابِهِ : هَلْ تَفْقِدُونَ مِنْ أَحَدٍ ؟ . قَالُوا : نَفْقِدُ فُلَانًا وَ نَفْقِدُ فُلَانًا . قَالَ : انْظُرْ هَلْ تَفْقِدُونَ مِنْ أَحَدٍ ؟ ، قَالُوا : لَا . قَالَ : لَكِنِّي أَفْقِدُ جُلَيْبِيبًا ، قَالَ : فَاطْلُبُوهُ فِي الْقَتْلَى . قَالَ : فَطَلَبُوهُ فَوَجَدُوهُ إِلَى جنبِ سَبْعَة قَدْ قَتَلَهُمْ ، ثُمَّ قَتَلُوهُ ، فَأَتَاهُ النَّبِيُّ صَلَّى اللهُ عَلَيْهِ وَ سَلَّمَ فَقَامَ عَلَيْهِ فَقَالَ :((قَتَلَ سَبْعَةً وَ قَتَلُوهُ، هَذَا مِنِّي وَ أَنَا مِنْهُ، هَذَا مِنِّي وَ أَنَا مِنْهُ)) مَرَّتَيْنِ أَوْ ثَلَاثًا ، ثُمَّ وَضَعَهُ رَسُولُ اللهِ صَلَّى اللهُ عَلَيْهِ وَ سَلَّمَ عَلَى سَاعِدَيْهِ وَ حفر لَهُ، مَا لَهُ سَرِيرٌ إِلَّا سَاعِدَا رَسُول اللهِ صَلَّى اللهُ عَلَيْهِ وَ سَلَّمَ، ثُمَّ وَضَعَهُ فِي قَبْرِهِ ، وَ لَمْ يَذْكُرْ أَنَّهُ غَسَّلَهُ .

قَالَ ثَابِتٌ : فَمَا كَانَ فِي الْأَنْصَارِ أَيِّمٌ أَنفق مِنْهَا . وَ حَدَّثَ إِسْحَاقُ بْنُ عَبْدِ اللهِ بن أَبِي طَلْحَةَ ثَابِتًا قَالَ : هَلْ تَعْلَمُ مَا دَعَا لَهَا رَسُولُ اللهِ صَلَّى اللهُ عَلَيْهِ وَ سَلَّمَ ؟ قَالَ : ((اللَّهُمَّ صُبَّ عَلَيْهَا الْخَيْرَ صَبًّا ، وَ لَا تَجْعَلْ عَيْشَهَا كَدًّا كَدًّا)) ، قَالَ : فَمَا كَانَ فِي الْأَنْصَارِ أَيِّمٌ أَنفق مِنْهَا .

"Julaybib was a man who used to come to women and joke with them. I said to my wife, 'Do not let Julaybib come to you, for if he does, I shall do such and such.' On another note, if any of the Ansar had a single female relative, they would not arrange a marriage for her until they found out whether the Prophet wants to marry her or not. The Prophet said to one of the Ansār: "Give me your daughter for marriage." He said, 'Yes, O Messenger of Allāh, it would be an honor and a blessing.' He said, "I do not want her for myself." He said, 'Then for whom, O Messenger of Allāh.'

He said, "For Julaybib." The man responded, 'O Messenger of Allāh, let me consult her mother.' So he went to the girl's mother and said, 'The Messenger of Allāh is proposing marriage for your daughter.' She said, 'Yes, it would be a pleasure.' He said, 'He is not proposing to marry her himself, he is proposing on behalf of Julaybib.'

She said, 'What! Julaybib No, by Allāh, we will not marry her to him.' When he wanted to get up and go to the Messenger of Allāh to tell him what the girl's mother had said, the girl asked, 'Who is asking for my hand' So her mother told her, and she said, 'Are you refusing to follow the command of the Messenger of Allāh. Follow his command, for I will not come to any harm.' So her father went to the Messenger of Allāh and said, 'Deal with her as you wish.' So he married her to Julaybib.

Then the Messenger of Allāh went out on one of his military campaigns, and after Allāh had granted him victory, he said to his Companions, may Allāh be pleased with them, "See whether

there is anybody missing." They said, 'We have lost so-and-so, and so-and-so.' He said, "See if there is anybody missing." They said, 'No one.' He said: "But I see that Julaybib is missing." He said: "Go and look for him among the dead." So they looked for him and found him beside seven of the enemy whom he had killed before he was himself killed. They said, 'O Messenger of Allāh, here he is, beside seven of the enemy whom he had killed before he was himself killed.' The Messenger of Allāh came and stood beside him and said, "He killed seven before he was himself killed. He belongs to me, and I belong to him." He said this two or three times, and then the Messenger of Allāh carried him in his arms and held him while his grave was dug, and then he placed him in his grave. It was not mentioned that he washed him, (رَضِيَ ٱللَّهُ عَنْهُ)."

Thābit (رَضِيَ ٱللَّهُ عَنْهُ) said: "There was no widow among the Ansār who was more sought after for marriage than that girl." 'Isḥāq bin 'Abdullāh bin Abī Talhah asked Thābit, "Do you know how the Messenger of Allāh prayed for that girl" He told

him: "He said, "O Allāh, pour blessings upon her and do not make her life hard." Moreover, this is how it was; there was no widow among the Ansār who was more sought after for marriage than her."[20]

al-Ḥāfidh Abū ʿUmar bin ʿAbdul al-Barr mentioned in al-Istiʿāb that when the girl said in her seclusion, "Are you refusing to follow the command of the Messenger of Allāh" This Ayah was revealed:

﴿ وَمَا كَانَ لِمُؤْمِنٍ وَلَا مُؤْمِنَةٍ إِذَا قَضَى ٱللَّهُ وَرَسُولُهُۥٓ أَمْرًا أَن يَكُونَ لَهُمُ ٱلْخِيَرَةُ مِنْ أَمْرِهِمْ ﴾

"It is not for a believer, man or woman when Allāh and His Messenger have decreed a matter that they should have any option in their decision."[21] [*Sūrah al-Ahzab* 33:32]

---

[20] - Recorded by Ahmad: (33/28).
[21] - Al-Istiʿāb: (131).

CHAPTER 3: THE SISTER'S ROLE IN ADVISING HER SIBLINGS

Siblings, whether in the same age or different, are mostly bound in a close-knitted group especially if they are adults. Interestingly, you may find two groups, the brothers group and the sisters group in the house; It appears so clearly when all the family members go to sleep. In such situation, the sisters share their secrets; and even the younger brother would approach his older sister in order to release his grief, worries, and other life tests and hardships he encounters. A wise sister should seize this opportunity of her siblings' feelings and give them the feeling she is their advisor and trustee. She should not by any means disclose any of their secrets to the other family members after they trusted her because this ought to make her lose their trust unless it is necessary for learning the proper way of advising them and make them realize their mistakes.

She should offer her advice and instructions to her siblings whenever she notices slackness in acts of worship, interactions, and morals especially if she is the oldest, most knowledgeable, and most religiously committed. On another level, the very advice the sister provides potentially commands people's respect and veneration especially males. It is very common that many people believe that males are more entitled to advise and guidance than females; this certainly is a misconception and invalid generalization. To prove this point, ʿĀishah once reproved her older brother's (ʿAbdur-Raḥmān ibn Abī Bakr) imperfection of Wuḍūʾ and advised to observe the Wuḍūʾ of the Prophet. Sālim, the freed slave of Shaddād, said:

دَخَلْتُ عَلَى عَائِشَةَ زَوْجِ النَّبِيِّ صَلَّى اللهُ عَلَيْهِ وَ سَلَّمَ يَوْمَ تُوُفِّيَ سَعْدُ بْنُ أَبِي وَقَّاصٍ ، فَدَخَلَ عَبْدُ الرَّحْمَنِ بْنِ أَبِي بَكر فَتَوَضَّأَ عِنْدَهَا ، فَقَالَتْ : يَا عَبْدَ الرَّحْمَنِ ! أَسْبِغِ الْوُضُوءَ ؛ فَإِنِّي سَمِعْتُ رَسُولَ اللهِ صَلَّى اللهُ عَلَيْهِ وَ سَلَّمَ يَقُولُ : ((وَيْلٌ لِلأَعْقَابِ مِنَ النَّارِ)).

"I came to ʿĀishah, the wife of the Prophet (صَلَّى ٱللَّهُ عَلَيْهِ وَسَلَّمَ), on the day when Sʿad bin Abī Waqqās died. ʿAbdur-Raḥmān bin Abū Bakr also came there, and he performed ablution in her presence. She said: ʿAbdur-Raḥmān, perfect the ablution as I heard Allāh's Messenger (صَلَّى ٱللَّهُ عَلَيْهِ وَسَلَّمَ) say: Woe to the heels because of the hell-fire."[22]

On another incident, she (ʿĀishah) rebuked him once she learned he favors one of his wives over the rest. az-Zubayr ibn Bakkār narrated from Hishām ibn Urwah from his father:

"ʿAbdur-Raḥmān bin Abī Bakr as-Ṣiddīq went to ash-Shām for conducting some business. He saw there a woman called: the daughter of al-Judi mounting on a bedding on the top of a camel surrounded by its babies. He liked this woman and composed some poetic verses:

"I thought of Laylā with as-Samawah[23] intervening between,

---

[22] - Recorded by Muslim: (240).

[23] - A name of a desert located in Syria, which was part of ash-Shām at that time. (Translator's note).

And what has the daughter of al-Judi (Laylā) to do with me."

He continued: when ʿUmar ibn al-Khaṭṭāb sent his army to ash-Shām, he commanded his army leader to bring Laylā, the daughter of al-Judi, if he wins and then send her to ʿAbdur-Raḥmān bin Abī Bakr. He did win and sent her to ʿAbdur-Raḥmān, who liked her and favored her over all of his wives so much they had to complain to ʿĀishah about him. ʿĀishah rebuked him for such thing. He told her, 'By Allāh, I almost feel like I eat pomegranate with her own teeth (expressing his love for her)." Laylā later suffered from a serious illness in her mouth, which drove ʿAbdur-Raḥmān to desert her until she complained to ʿĀishah about him. ʿĀishah advised him,

يَا عَبْدَ الرَّحْمَنِ ، لَقَدْ أَحَبَبْتَ لَيْلَى فَأَفْرَطْتَ ، وَ أَبْغَضْتَهَا فَأَفْرَطْتَ ، فَإِمَّا أَنْ تُنْصِفَهَا ، وَ إِمَّا أَنْ تُجَهِّزَهَا إِلَى أَهْلِهَا ، فَجَهَّزَهَا إِلَى أَهْلِهَا .

"ʿAbdur-Raḥmān, you have been infatuated with Laylā (for some time) but also you have disliked

**her to the extreme; so, either you be fair with her
or send her back to her folks." At last, he sent her
to her folks."[24]**

Likewise, Ḥafṣah, daughter of ʿUmar ibn al-Khaṭṭāb, did
the same thing with her brother ʿAbdullāh ibn ʿUmar
during the time of the great discord among the Muslims.
She advised him to commit to al-Jamāʿah (the
mainstream of Muslims) and never disobey the supreme
ruler of the Muslims. Her advice to her brothers spared
bloodshed.

Ibn ʿUmar said,

دَخَلْتُ عَـلَى حَـفْصَـةَ وَ نَسْوَاتُهَا تَنْطُفُ، قُلْتُ: قَدْ

كَـانَ مِـنْ أَمْرِ النَّـاسِ مَا تَرَيْنَ فَلَـمْ يَجْعَـلْ لِي مِنَ الْأَمْرِ

شَيْءٌ، فَقَـالَتْ: اِلْحَـقْ فَإِنَّهُـمْ يَنْتَظِـرُونَكَ، وَ أَخْـشَى

أَنْ يَكُـونَ فِي احْتِبَاسِكَ عَنْهُـمْ فُرْقَةٌ، فَلَـمْ تَدَعُهُ حَتَّى

ذَهَبَ، فَلَمَّا تَفَرَّقَ النَّـاسُ خَطَبَ مُعَاوِيَةُ، قَالَ: مَنْ

---

24 - Taḥdhīb al-Kamāl: (16/558).

كَانَ يُرِيدُ أَنْ يَتَكَلَّمَ فِي هَذَا الأَمْرِ فَلْيُطْلِعَ لَنَا قرنَهُ ، فَلَنَحْنُ أَحَقُّ بِهِ مِنْهُ وَ مِنْ أَبِيهِ ؛ قَالَ حَبِيبٌ بْنُ مسلمة : فَهَلَّا أَجَبْتَهُ ؟ قَالَ عَبْدُ الله : فَحَلَلْتُ حُبْوَتِي وَ هَمَمْتُ أَنْ أَقُولَ : أَحَقُّ بِهَذَا الأَمْرِ مِنْكَ مَنء قَاتَلَكَ وَ أَبَاكَ عَلَى الْإِسْلَامِ ، فَخَشِيتُ أَنْ أَقُولَ كَلِمَةً تُفَرِّقُ بَيْنَ الْجَمْعِ وَ تَسفكُ الدَّمَ ، وَ يُحْمَلُ عَنِّي غَيْر ذَلِكَ ، فَذَكَرْتُ مَا أَعَدَّ اللهُ فِي الْجَنَانِ . قَالَ حَبِيبٌ : ((حُفِظْتَ وَ عُصِمْتَ)) .

"I went to Ḥafṣah while water was dribbling from her twined braids. I said, 'The condition of the people is as you see, and no authority has been given to me.' Ḥafṣah said, (to me), 'Go to them, and as they (i.e. the people) are waiting for you, and I am afraid your absence from them will cause division amongst them.' "So Ḥafṣah did not leave Ibn ʿUmar till we went to them.

When the people differed, Muʿāwiyah addressed the people saying,

> **"'If anybody wants to say anything in this matter of the Caliphate, he should show up and not conceal himself, for we are more rightful to be a Caliph than he and his father."**

On that, Ḥabīb bin Masalamah said (to Ibn ʿUmar),

> **"Why don't you reply to him (i.e. Muʿāwiyah)?" ʿAbdullāh bin ʿUmar said, "I untied my garment that was going round my back and legs while I was sitting and was about to say, 'He who fought against you and your father for the sake of Islām, is more rightful to be a Caliph,' but I was afraid that my statement might produce differences amongst the people and cause bloodshed, and my statement might be misinterpreted. (So I kept quiet) remembering what Allāh has prepared in the Gardens of Paradise (for those who are patient and prefer the Hereafter to this worldly life).**

> **"Ḥabīb said, "You did what kept you safe and secure (i.e. you were wise in doing so)."[25]**

Al-Ḥāfiẓ Ibn Ḥajr commented,

> **"Ibn ʿUmar was referring to the battle that took place in Siffin between ʿAli and Muʿāwiyah, when they agreed to settle their differences and sent mail to the rest of the companions residing in al-Haramayn and elsewhere. They agreed to meet in order to settle it. Ibn ʿUmar consulted his sister regarding his attendance at the meeting; should he go or not? She advised him to go lest his absence would potentially deepen the discord."[26]**

Ibn al-Mulaqqin noted,

> **"Ḥafṣah drew his attention (to the fact) that his absence will definitely create division."[27]**

---

[25] - Recorded by al-Bukhārī: (4108).
[26] - Fath al-Bari: (9/199).
[27] - Al-Tawdeeh fee Sharh al-Jāmiʿ as-Ṣaḥīḥ: (21/234).

CHAPTER 4: THE WIFE'S ROLE IN ADVISING HER HUSBAND

The marital bond is a strong one and the sturdiest because both couples live most of their lives together. They are even more like a garment for each other. Allāh says,

﴿ هُنَّ لِبَاسٌ لَّكُمْ وَأَنتُمْ لِبَاسٌ لَّهُنَّ ﴾

"They are your cover, and you are their cover." [*Sūrah al-Baqarah* 2:187]

Ibn Kathīr commented,

وَ حَاصِلُهُ أَنَّ الرَّجُلَ وَ الْمَرْأَةَ كُلٌّ مِنْهُمَا يُخَالِطُ الْآخَرَ وَ يُمَاسُّهُ وَ يُضَاجِعُهُ .

"In short, the wife and the husband are intimate and have sexual intercourse with each other."[28]

If that is so, there is no doubt that the wife knows her husband more than anybody else. She knows his true character, traits, morals, worship, commitment to obedience, and she can advise him whenever she notices negligence in his religious commitment or his integrity. This makes her a huge support for him in worshipping Allāh and getting closer to Him, and the only way to achieve this is by offering her advice since people with closer relations are more entitled to the advice than those with far relations; and who is closer to the husband than his wife?!

ʿĀishah (may Allāh be pleased with her) used to teach women and instruct them to advise their husbands. Muʿādhah narrated that ʿĀishah said:

[28] - Tafsīr ibn Kathīr: 2/194).

مُرْنَ أَزْوَاجَكُنَّ أَنْ يَسْتَطِيبُوا بِالْمَاءِ فَإِنِّي أَسْتَحِييهُمْ ، فَإِنَّ رَسُولَ اللهِ صَلَّى اللهُ عَلَيْهِ وَ سَلَّمَ كَانَ يَفْعَلُهُ .

"Tell your husbands to clean themselves with water, for I am too shy to tell them myself. The Messenger of Allāh (ﷺ) used to do that."[29]

Al-ʿAllāmah Muḥammad al-Mukhṭār al-Shinqīṭī (d.1405 A.H.) remarked,

فِيهِ دَلِيلٌ أَنَّ الْمَرْأَةَ تَأْمُرُ زَوْجَهَا وَ تَنْهَاهُ إِذَا عَلِمَتْ مِنْ أَمْرِ الدُّنْيَا مَا يَجْهَلُهُ ، وَ كَذَلِكَ تَبْذُلُ لَهُ النَّصِيحَةَ فِيمَا تَرَاهُ خَيْرًا لَهُ .

"This Ḥadīth proves that the wife is permitted to instruct her husband to do or not to do if she knows a religious matter he is ignorant of as well

29 - Recorded by al-Tirmidhī: (19).

as offers her advice to him at whatever she considers best for him."[30]

The wife's advice to her husband will positively lead to more affability and intimacy between them. It also proves her love, care, and desire for him to be all good whether this advice is related to something religious or worldly since they are all a part of advice.

For instance, 'Umm Salamah offered a very sound advice to the Prophet at Hudaybīyah related to the way he should deal with his companions about making 'Iḥlāl from 'Umrah.

az-Zuhrī related that al-Miswār bin Makhramah and Marwan (whose narrations attest each other) narrated that Allāh's Messenger (صَلَّىٱللَّهُعَلَيْهِوَسَلَّمَ) set out at the time of al-Hudaybiyah (treaty).'

Al-Bukhārī recorded the whole story including,

[30] - Shurūq 'Anwār al-Minān: (1/280).

فَلَمَّا فَرَغَ مِنْ قَضِيَّةِ الْكِتَابِ، قَالَ رَسُولُ اللهِ صَلَّى اللهُ عَلَيْهِ وَ سَلَّمَ لِأَصْحَابِهِ: ((قُومُوا فَانْحَرُوا ثُمَّ احْلِقُوا)).

"When the writing of the peace treaty was concluded, Allāh's Messenger (ﷺ) said to his companions,

"Get up and slaughter your sacrifices and get your head shaved."

By Allāh, none of them got up, and the Prophet repeated his order thrice. When none of them got up, he left them and went to ʾUmm Salamah and told her of the people's attitudes towards him. ʾUmm Salamah said,

يَا نَبِيَّ اللهِ! أَ تُحِبُّ ذَلِكَ، اخْرُجْ ثُمَّ لَا تُكَلِّمْ أَحَدًا مِنْهُمْ كَلِمَةً حَتَّى تَنْحَرَ بُدْنَكَ وَ تَدْعُو حَالِقَكَ فَيَحْلُقَكَ، فَخَرَجَ فَلَمْ يُكَلِّمْ أَحَدًا مِنْهُمْ حَتَّى فَعَلَ

ذَلِكَ ، نَحَرَ بُدْنَهُ وَ دَعَا حَالِقَهُ فَحَلَقَهُ ، فَلَمَّا رَأَوْا ذَلِكَ قَامُوا فَنَحَرُوا ، وَ جَعَلَ بَعْضُهُمْ يَحْلُقُ بَعْضًا حَتَّى كَانَ بَعْضُهُمْ يَقْتُلُ بَعْضًا غَمًّا ...

"O the Prophet (صَلَّى ٱللَّٰهُ عَلَيْهِ وَسَلَّمَ) of Allāh! Do you want your order to be carried out? Go out and don't say a word to anybody till you have slaughtered your sacrifice and call your barber to shave your head." So, the Prophet (صَلَّى ٱللَّٰهُ عَلَيْهِ وَسَلَّمَ) went out and did not talk to anyone of them till he did that, i.e. slaughtered the sacrifice and called his barber who shaved his head. Seeing that, the companions of the Prophet (صَلَّى ٱللَّٰهُ عَلَيْهِ وَسَلَّمَ) got up, slaughtered their sacrifices, and started shaving the heads of one another, and there was so much rush that there was a danger of killing each other."[31]

Al-Ḥāfiẓ Ibn Ḥajr commented,

"It is possible that ʾUmm Salamah thought of the companions to have deemed the Prophet's

---

31 - Recorded by al-Bukhārī: (2731).

command to make ʾIḥlāl as a concession for them while he would still keep his ʾIḥrām without taking the concession. So, she advised him to make ʾIḥlāl in order for the companions to dismiss their thought. The Prophet knew what she advised was right and he done it. After that, when the companions saw the Prophet, they rushed to do what they were commanded since they had no reason to wait. This Ḥadīth reflects the virtue of consulting and that one's words if confirmed by his action is more effective than mere words.

It does not, however, imply that action is more effective than words in all aspects. Furthermore, it contains the permissibility of consulting the virtuous woman as well as highlighting the virtue of ʾUmm Salamah and her formidable intellect. Imām al-Haramin complemented her, "ʾUmm Salamah is the only lady we know of who offered an opinion which was right." This is his statement; however, some reconsidered his

statement and added the daughter of Shuʿayb when (she advised her father) about Mūsā."[32]

On the other hand, if the wife ignored advising her husband when she notices a considerable negligence in his religious commitment, morals, or dealings, this is considered some kind of betrayal to him let alone she could be the reason he engages in unlawful deeds and wrongdoings. The Proof is found in the Ḥadīth where Abu Hurayrah narrated that the Prophet (صَلَّى ٱللَّهُ عَلَيْهِ وَسَلَّمَ) said,

لَوْ لَا بَنُو إِسْرَائِيلَ لَمْ يَخْنَزِ اللَّحْمُ، وَ لَوْ لَا حَوَّاءُ لَمْ تَخُنْ أُنْثَى زَوْجَهَا الدَّهْرَ.

"Were it not for Banī Isrāʾīl, meat would not decay; and were it not for Eve, no woman would ever betray her husband."[33]

Imām Ibn Hubayrah said,

"Eve's betrayal of her husband was when she had not advised him against eating from the tree after

[32] - Fatḥ al-Barī: (6/864).
[33] - Recorded by al-Bukhārī: (3330- 3399) and Muslim: (1470).

he decided to eat from it. This is considered a betrayal. As a result, anyone who sees his brother involved in wrongdoing without advising him, this would be a betrayal of him."[34]

In the Encyclopedia of the Muslim family, it says,

"When Eve noticed the weakness of ʾĀdam, she actually made him, even more, weak as she did not express any disapproval and hence he committed the violation. Appropriately speaking, a good wife should not remain silent nor commend any form of wrongdoing her husband engages in. Instead, she should advise him gently over and over (even if it requires) applying all the necessary pressure. She should employ all of the emotional, mental, and physical strategies at her disposal exactly as she strives in asking for her rights and personal needs. She must do her best in rectifying her husband if he disobeyed his

---

34 - Al-ʾIfṣāḥ ʿan Mʿānī aṣ-Ṣihāh: (7/230).

parents, abandoned prayer, or intermingled with evil people."[35]

In a nutshell, the righteous believing woman assists her husband in his religious and faith affairs. She has a powerful influence to sway her husband's course; so, obviously, she should sway him to do good instead of bad. The Prophet addressed women,

مَا رَأَيْتُ مِنْ نَاقِصَاتِ عَقْلٍ وَ دِينٍ أَذْهَبَ لِلُبِّ الرَّجُلِ الْحَازِمِ مِنْ إِحْدَاكُنَّ يَا مَعْشَرَ النِّسَاءِ.

"I have not seen anyone more deficient in intelligence and religion than you, who is capable of muddling the mindsight[36] **of a resolved man."**[37]

---

35 - "The encyclopedia of the Muslim family" al-Mawsūʿah al-Shāmilah.

36 - **Translator's note**: "**mindsight**" is: a term coined by Dr. Dan Siegel, a professor of psychiatry at UCLA school of Medicine, to describe our human capacity to perceive the mind of the self and others. It is a powerful lens through which we can understand our inner lives with more clarity, integrate the brain, and enhance our relationships with others.

37 - Recorded by al-Bukhārī: (1462) and Muslim: (889).

So, given that a woman is influential enough to sway a resolved man from good to evil, she should key in bringing about the good and fending off evil. In addition, she should sway a reckless man to do good by means of offering advice and instructions. Al-Ḥāfiẓ Ibn Ḥajr said,

> **"The word 'muddle' is to emphasize the impact of her influence; 'mindsight' is more specific than just mind as it is the inner core of it. The word 'resolved' refers to the person who is in total control of his self. The Ḥadīth overstates their description, since if they are influential enough to swerve a resolved man, it is all the more reason they would be even more influential on an unresolved man."**[38]

So, obviously, an advising woman is a priceless opportunity one should seize for himself; she is, even more, precious than silver and gold. Thawbān narrated:

[38] - Fatḥ al-Barī: (1/688).

لَـمَّـا نَـزَلَـتْ ﴿ وَٱلَّذِينَ يَكۡنِزُونَ ٱلذَّهَبَ وَٱلۡفِضَّـةَ ﴾

قَـالَ: كُـنَّـا مَـعَ الـنَّـبِـيِّ صَـلَّـى اللهُ عَـلَـيْـهِ وَ سَـلَّـمَ فِـي بَـعْـضِ

أَسْـفَـارِهِ ، فَـقَـالَ بَـعْـضُ أَصْـحَـابِـهِ : أُنْـزِلَـتْ فِـي الـذَّهَـبِ وَ

الْـفِـضَّـةِ ، لَـوْ عَـلِـمْـنَـا أَيُّ الْـمَـالِ خَـيْـرٌ فَـنَـتَّـخِـذَهُ؟ فَـقَـالَ :

((أَفْـضَـلُـهُ لِـسَـانٌ ذَاكِـرٌ ، وَ قَـلْـبٌ شَـاكِـرٌ ، وَ زَوْجَـةٌ مُـؤْمِـنَـةٌ

تُـعِـيـنُـهُ عَـلَـى إِيـمَـانِـهِ)).

"When (the following) was revealed:

"And those who hoard up gold and silver..." [*Sūrah at-Tawbah* 9:34]

He said:

"We were with the Messenger of Allāh (صَلَّى ٱللَّهُ عَلَيْهِ وَسَلَّمَ) during one of his journeys, so some of his Companions said: (This) has been revealed about gold and silver, if we knew which wealth was better, then we would use it. So he (صَلَّى ٱللَّهُ عَلَيْهِ وَسَلَّمَ) said: 'The most virtuous of it is a remembering tongue,

a grateful heart, and a believing wife that helps him with his faith.'"[39]

[39] - Recorded by al-Tirmidhī: (3094), ibn Mājah in as-Sunnan: (1856) and it is authenticated by al-Albānī in as-Silsilah as-Ṣaḥīḥah: (2176).

SECTION 2: ADVISING OUTSIDE HOUSE AND ITS METHODS

Introduction:

It is mentioned in the first chapter that a woman should be settling home, as she is the mother, educator, and the one who takes care of her house. She can go outside her house if there are unanticipated contingent circumstances. There is not a single instruction in the Sharīʿah of Allāh that disallows women to never go outside their houses. Totally the opposite, she is allowed to go outside in accordance with the Sharīʿah guidelines laid down in the Book of Allāh and the Sunnah of His Prophet. This book, however, is not purposed to cite those guidelines. It is rather purposed to explore the various means of advice a woman can do outside her house; since she is bound to go outside for multiple reasons. There are various proofs from the Sunnah that prove this point.

Jābir bin ʿAbdullāh (رَضِيَ اللَّهُ عَنْهُمَا) reported:

طُلِّقَتْ خَالَتِي فَأَرَادَتْ أَنْ تَجُدَّ نَخْلَهَا فَزَجَرَهَا رَجُلٌ أَنْ تَخْرُجَ ، فَأَتَتِ النَّبِيَّ صَلَّى اللهُ عَلَيْهِ وَ سَلَّمَ فَقَالَ : ((بَلَى فَجُدِّي نَخْلَكِ ، فَإِنَّكِ عَسَى أَنْ تَصَدَّقِي أَنْ تَفْعَلِي مَعْرُوفًا)).

My maternal aunt was divorced, and she intended to pluck her dates. A person scolded her for having come out (during the period of ʿIdda). She came to Allāh's Prophet (صَلَّى اللَّهُ عَلَيْهِ وَسَلَّمَ) and he said:

"Certainly you can pluck (dates) from your palm trees, for perhaps you may give charity or do an act of kindness."[40]

Moreover, she can go out to perform Allāh's obligations, to listen to Dhikr, learn, and teach in the Masājid or elsewhere. The Prophet (صَلَّى اللَّهُ عَلَيْهِ وَسَلَّمَ) ordered that they

---

40 - Recorded by Muslim: (1483).

must not be prevented from going to the Masjid. Ibn ʿUmar (رَضِيَ اللَّهُ عَنْهُ) said:

كَانَتْ امْرَأَةٌ لِعُمَرَ تَشْهَدُ صَلَاةَ الصُّبْحِ وَ الْعِشَاءِ فِي الْجَمَاعَةِ فِي الْمَسْجِدِ، فَقِيلَ لَهَا: لِمَ تَخْرُجِينَ وَ قَدْ تَعْلَمِينَ أَنَّ عُمَرَ يَكْرَهُ ذَلِكَ وَ يَغَارُ؟ قَالَتْ: وَ مَا يَمْنَعُهُ أَنْ يَنْهَانِي؟ قَالَ: يَمْنَعُ قَوْلُ رَسُولِ اللهِ صَلَّى اللهُ عَلَيْهِ وَ سَلَّمَ: ((لَا تَمْنَعُوا إِمَاءَ اللهِ مَسَاجِدَ اللهِ)).

"One of the wives of ʿUmar (bin al-Khaṭṭāb) used to offer the Fajr and the ʿIshāʾ prayer in congregation in the Masjid. She was asked why she had come out for the prayer as she knew that 'Umar disliked it and that he gets jealous. She replied, "What prevents him from stopping me from this act?" The other replied, "The statement of Allāh's Messenger (صَلَّى اللَّهُ عَلَيْهِ وَسَلَّمَ): 'Do not prevent Allāh's women-servants from going to Allāh's Masājid (i.e., plural for Masjid)."[41]

---

41 - Recorded by al-Bukhārī: (900) and Muslim: (442).

In another narration, it says,

وَ لَكِنْ لِيَخْرُجْنَ وَ هُنَّ تَفِلَاتٌ

"but they may go out (to the Masjid) having not perfumed themselves."[42]

Since that is the case, then the woman ought to know her obligations when she is outside the house with her fellow women at any place she could be; be that at the Masjid, workplace, study place, or elsewhere where she most often goes in accordance with Sharīʿah guidelines. One of the foremost obligations is offering advice for others. A woman intermingles with many different types of women. She will see or hear violations of Allāh's Sharīʿah. Moreover, a woman who is desirous to do good would be a caller to Allāh wherever she is; she offers directions, education, and advice in order to please her Lord as well as out of a desire to guide her fellow women. She should never lose sight of the Prophet's saying,

[42] - Recorded by Abū Dāwud: (565).

SECTION 2: ADVISING OUTSIDE HOUSE AND ITS METHODS

الـدِّيـنُ الـنَّـصِـيـحَـةُ

"The religion is advice."[43]

Moreover, also his saying,

وَالـنُّـصْـحِ لِـكُـلِّ مُـسْـلِـمٍ

"Advice is for every Muslim."[44]

The following chapters demonstrate how the woman should be outside her house. There are examples from the early Salafī women that explore their dealings with others in terms of offering advice, instructions, and guidance.

---

43 - Recorded by Muslim: (55).

44 - Recorded by al-Bukhārī (57) and Muslim: (56).

CHAPTER 5: ADVISING INSIDE THE STUDY PLACE

Undoubtedly, educating girls has its very fruitful results that benefit the Islāmic nation whereas ignoring it harms them. Such fact is out of the question by any rational man. The following poetic verses expound on this point. In a friendly advice given by Shaykh Muḥammad al-Bashir al-ʾIbrāhīmī to Shaykh Muḥammad ibn ʾIbrāhīm Āli ash-Shaykh (may Allāh have mercy on both of them). The advice explains the level of education and knowledge a young girl should be at instead of depriving her of reading and learning, which only brings about disasters on the Islāmic nation.

He said:

Between us, there are some pieces of advice needed to be reminded,

Concealing them is cowardice, cheating, and harm,

Never forget about Eve, as she is the sister of the male,

Inside her is good and evil just like him,

Bears sweet and bitter fruits just like him

The (quality) of her fruit is dependent on how she is instituted

Whatever you instill in her shall be settled within,

So how could a rational man be pleased to leave her

Useless and with no avail,

In her youth, you plant in her seeds of corruption,

Melting in her morals along with virtue,

If she were to be left out,

Disaster, destruction, and harm are bound to happen,

However, if she were to be educated, she would be an asset,

Alternatively, a sin bringing nothing but bad outcome,

To prevent her from learning (is unauthorized) as not a shred of evidence (a verse or report) is reported,

(Heed the example of) the virtuous women of the past age (Salaf)

Grateful is what they are

Think, may Allāh guide you, what is to be expected

Of a nation whose half is paralyzed by laziness,

Think! It is possible that thinking might guide you,

And heed the lessons of time

Is there any of the great civilizations,

From the past or the present,

Who flourished with greatness and good history

Except by both males and females?

Whoever argues that evil and misguidance is in educating her

Tell him: she is, even more, evil if she is ignorant.[45]

So, when the girl goes to school in accordance with the Sharīʿah guidelines, it is obvious that she will spend a long time with her schoolmate girls. Some of them are righteous while others are negligent of Allāh's commands and commit wrongdoings. A righteous girl seizes this opportunity and makes Daʿwah and offers her advice throughout school grades. She should plan a strategy for treating, advising others, and guiding them to their mistakes. If she sees a girl whose clothes expresses a lack of decency and modesty, she should advise her and explain to her the virtue of Ḥijāb and that it pleases Allāh; in addition to fending off evil and harm.

Likewise, if she sees other girls who are blinded by what the unchaste western women have and followed them in their way of dressing, hairstyle, or anything else, she should warn them against following the steps of the Shayṭān and the disbelievers in their every move. She should also make it clear to her that the Muslim woman

---

[45] - Athar ash-Shaykh Muḥammad al-Bashir al-ʾIbrāhīmī: (4/133).

has her own independent personality that induces her with the kind of pride that brings her closer to Her Creator.

Advice should be offered by all means necessary at her disposal; directly or indirectly. Sometimes a course of conversation is to be taken, while other times some tapes, booklets, or beneficial pamphlets related to Daʿwah are to be presented to whoever is ignorant of the advantages and beauty of the religion of Islām. Achieving this would mean that she has fulfilled her part in advice and secures a spot for her among those whom the Prophet described,

الدَّالُّ عَلَى الْخَيْرِ كَفَاعِلِهِ

"Whoever guides to good is the same as the one who does it."[46]

46 - Recorded by al-Tirmidhī: (2667) ad authenticated by al-Albānī in as-Ṣaḥīḥah: (1660).

CHAPTER 6: THE WOMAN'S ROLE IN ADVISING IN HER LOCAL MASJID

It has been mentioned earlier some of the Narrations where the Prophet (صَلَّى ٱللَّهُ عَلَيْهِ وَسَلَّمَ) permitted for women to go out to the Masjid whether it is for praying in congregation or for learning knowledge. A woman is definitely going to meet other women of different age groups; old ladies, adults, and girl youngsters. Hence, she must take into consideration their age and mind differential in advising them pertaining any wrongdoing they commit. Particularly, when women gather in one place, they tend to be chatty; and Shayṭān may potentially induce them until they are trapped in gossip, backbiting, and ill talk about others.

Some of them bring their children but poorly educate them to cut disrupting those who are engaged in praying and Dhikr. Others engage in conversation while the Imām is delivering his Jumuʿah speech. This requires the woman who advises to be perceptive and employs wisdom in righting these wrong practices that consistently take place in the Masjid. She could either deal with those problems directly and advise her fellow women or report those practices to the Imām of the Masjid. He, in return, would clarify those issues; and this could be received with more responsive welcoming.

For instance, some of the mothers of believers used to forbid evil inside the houses of Allāh, and advice whoever is involved in wrongdoing. Mujāhid reported:

دَخَلْتُ أَنَا وَ عُرْوَةُ بْنُ الزُّبَيْرِ الْمَسْجِدَ فَإِذَا عَبْدُ اللهِ ابْنِ عُمَرَ رَضِيَ اللهُ عَنْهُمَا جَالِسٌ إِلَى حجرَةِ عَائِشَةَ، وَ إِذَا نَاسٌ يُصَلُّونَ فِي الْمَسْجِدِ صَلَاةَ الضُّحَى ، قَالَ : فَسَأَلْنَاهُ عَنْ صَلَاتِهِمْ ، فَقَالَ : بِدْعَةٌ ، ثُمَّ قَالَ لَهُ : كَمْ اعْتَمَرَ رَسُولُ اللهِ صَلَّى اللهُ عَلَيْهِ وَ سَلَّمَ ؟ قَالَ : أَرْبَع ، إِحْدَاهُنَّ فِي رَجَبٍ ، فَكَرِهنَا أَنْ نَرُدَّ عَلَيْهِ . قَالَ : وَ سَمِعْنَا اِسْتَنَانَ عَائِشَةَ أُمِّ الْمُؤْمِنِينَ فِي الْحجرَةِ

فَقَالَ عُرْوَةُ : يَا أُمَّاه ! يَا أُمَّ الْمُؤْمِنِينَ ! أَ لَا تَسْمَعِينَ مَا يَقُولُ أَبُو عَبْدِ الرَّحْمَنِ ؟ قَالَتْ : مَا يَقُولُ ؟ قَالَ : يَقُولُ : إِنَّ رَسُولَ اللهِ صَلَّى اللهُ عَلَيْهِ وَ سَلَّمَ اعْتَمَرَ أَرْبَعَ عُمَرَاتٍ إِحْدَاهُنَّ فِي رَجَبٍ ، قَالَتْ : يَرْحَمُ اللهُ أَبَا عَبْدِ الرَّحْمَنِ ! مَا اعْتَمَرَ عُمْرَةً إِلَّا وَ هُوَ شَاهِدُهُ ، وَ مَا اعْتَمَرَ فِي رَجَبٍ قَطُّ .

ʿUrwah bin Zubayr and I entered the Masjid and found ʿAbdullāh bin ʿUmar sitting near the apartment of ʿĀishah and the people were observing the forenoon prayer (when the sun had sufficiently risen). We asked him about their prayer, and he said: It is Bidʿah (innovation), Urwah said to him: O Abū ʿAbdur Raḥmān, how many ʿUmrahs did Allāh's Messenger (ﷺ) perform? He said: "Four ʿUmrahs including one he performed during the month of Rajab."

We were reluctant either to believe him or reject him. We heard the noise of teeth brushing by

ʿĀishah in her apartment. ʿUrwah said: Mother of the Faithful, are you not hearing what Abī ʿAbdur-Raḥmān is saying? She said: What is he saying? Thereupon he ('Urwah) said: He (Ibn 'Umar) states that Allāh's Messenger (ﷺ) performed four ʿUmrahs and one of them during the month of Rajab. Thereupon she remarked:

"May Allāh have mercy upon Abū ʿAbdur al-Raḥmān. Never did Allāh's Messenger (ﷺ) perform ʿUmrah in which he did not accompany him, and he (Allāh's Messenger) never performed ʿUmrah during the month of Rajab."[47]

Additionally, she rebuked some of the young men's ridicule of a trialed man. She advised them to abandon this behavior. Aswad reported that some young men from the Quraysh visited ʿĀishah as she was in Mina and they were laughing. She said:

[47] -Recorded by al-Bukhārī: (1775-1776) and Muslim: (1255).

مَا يُضْحِكُكُمْ ؟ قَالُوا : فُلَانٌ خَرَّ عَلَى طُنب فسطَاطٍ فَكَادتْ عُنُقُهُ أَوْ عَيْنُهُ أَنْ تَذْهَبَ؛ فَقَالَتْ : لَا تَضْحَكُوا؛ فَإِنِّي سَمِعْتُ رَسُولَ الله صَلَّى اللهُ عَلَيْهِ وَ سَلَّمَ قَالَ : ((مَا مِنْ مُسْلِمٍ يُشَاكُ شَوْكَةً فَمَا فَوْقَهَا إِلَّا كُتِبَتْ لَه بِهَا دَرَجَةٌ ، وَ مُحِيَتْ عَنْهُ بِهَا خَطِيئَةٌ .((

"What makes you laugh? They said: Such and such person stumbled against the rope of the tent, and he was about to break his neck or lose his eyes. She said: Don't laugh for I heard Allāh's Messenger (ﷺ) as saying: "If a Muslim runs into a thorn or (gets into trouble) severe than this, there is assured for him (a higher) rank and his sins are obliterated."[48]

ʿUrwah Ibn Az-Zubayr said ʿĀishah reported:

---

[48] - Recorded by Muslim: (2572).

أَ لَا يعجبكَ أَبُو فُلَانٍ ، جَاءَ فَجَلَسَ إِلَى جَانِب حجرتِي يُحَدِّثُ عَنْ رَسُولِ اللهِ صَلَّى اللهُ عَلَيْهِ وَ سَلَّمَ يُسْمِعُنِي ذَلِكَ ، وَ كُنْتُ أُسَبِّحُ ، فَقَامَ قَبْلَ أَنْ أَقْضِي سُبْحَتِي ، وَ لَوْ أَدْرَكْتُهُ لَرَدَدْتُّ عَلَيْهِ ؛ إِنَّ رَسُولَ اللهِ صَلَّى اللهُ عَلَيْهِ وَ سَلَّمَ لَمْ يَكُنْ يسرُدُ الْحَدِيثَ كَسردِكُمْ .

"Don't you feel surprised at the father of so and so? He came (one day) and sat beside the corner of my apartment and began to narrate (the Ḥadīth of Allāh's Messenger). I was hearing while I was engaged in extolling Allāh (reciting Subhan Allāh) constantly. He stood up before I finished my repetition of Subhan Allāh. If I were to meet him, I would have warned him with stern words that Allāh's Messenger (ﷺ) did not speak so quickly as you talk."[49]

[49] - Recorded by al-Bukhārī: (3568) and Muslim: (2493).

Ibn Ḥajr commented.

> **"Her saying, 'I would have warned him with stern words' means she would have strongly reproached him and made it clear to him that the proper way of narrating a Ḥadīth is by reading it slowly better than quickly."**[50]

Moreover, ʿĀishah's story of reproaching who denounced performing the funeral prayer in the Masjid is famous. ʿĀishah reported that when Sʿad bin Abū Waqqās died, the wives of the Messenger of Allāh (ﷺ) sent message to bring his bier[51] into the Masjid so that they should offer the funeral prayer for him. They (the participants of the funeral) did accordingly, and it was placed in front of their apartments, and they offered prayer for him. It was brought out of the door (known as) Bab al-Janāʾiz which was towards the side of Maqāʾid, and the news reached them (the wives of the Prophet) that the people bad criticized this (i.e. offering of funeral prayer in the

[50] - Fatḥ al-Barī: (8/222).

[51] **Publisher's note:** the word **'bier'** by definition is a frame or stand on which a corpse or the coffin containing it is laid before burial.

masjid) saying that it was not desirable to take the bier inside the masjid. This was conveyed to ʿĀishah. She said:

مَـا أَسْـرَعَ الـنَّـاس إِلَـى أَنْ يَـعِـيـبُـوا مَـا لَا عِـلْـمَ لَـهُـمْ بِـهِ ، عَـابُـوا عَـلَـيْـنَـا أَنْ يُـمـرَّ بِـجَـنَـازَةٍ فِـي الْـمَـسْـجِـدِ ، وَ مَـا صَـلَّـى رَسُـولُ اللهِ صَـلَّـى اللهُ عَـلَـيْـهِ وَ سَـلَّـمَ عَـلَـى سُـهَـيْـلِ بْـن بَـيْـضَـاء إِلَّا فِـي جَـوْفِ الْـمَـسْـجِـدِ .

"How hastily the people criticize that about which they know little. They criticize us for carrying the bier in the masjid. The Messenger of Allāh (ﷺ) offered not the funeral prayer of Suhayl bin Baydaʿh but in the innermost part of the masjid."[52]

52 - Recorded by Muslim: (973).

CHAPTER 7: THE WOMAN'S ROLE IN ADVISING IN HER WORKPLACE

This chapter is not much different from the previous ones except that it informs the woman when she goes out to her workplace in accordance with the Sharīʿah guidelines, she will spend a long time with workmates; sometimes it may be up to more than six hours' long a day. Unfortunately, it is undoubted that staying such a long time not only provokes a weak response to wrongdoings inside the workplace but also creates a scenario where she could probably get used to (witnessing such wrongdoings) until she can no longer get her facts straight; the right will be wrong and vice versa.

Therefore, she is strongly advised to keep her facts and faith in regular check. She should display her refusal of the wrongdoings verbally and by her heart. In addition, she should advise those who engage in wrongdoing especially if she holds a position of multiple responsibilities. In this case, her obligation is, even more, pressing. For instance, she could be a school principal, a teacher, or an educator who raises the future generations of righteous Muslim girl youngsters. Given her position, she should seize the (advantage) of her social status in the best way she can manage in order to help others through advice and guidance because she occupies a respectable and admirable position.

She can connect with her fellow women through being a role model and by offering them advice and instructions. A woman, particularly, is vulnerable outside her house. The Shayṭān always seeks to tempt her, makes falsehood fair-seeming to her, and twists corruption with goodness.

ʿAbdullāh ibn Masʿūd narrated that The Prophet (ﷺ) said:

الْمَرْأَةُ عَوْرَةٌ، فَإِذَا خَرَجَتِ اسْتَشْرَفَهَا الشَّيْطَانُ

"The woman is Awrah, so when she goes out, the Shayṭān seeks to tempt her."[53]

There is an addition in another narration that says,

وَ إِنَّـهَـا لَا تَـكُـونُ إِلَـى وَجْـهِ الله أَقْـرَبَ مِـنْـهَـا فِـي قَـعْـرِ بَـيْـتِـهَـا

"And she is closest to Allāh when she stays in her house."[54]

One can observe that the woman who works outside her house is more susceptible to the whispers of both human and Jinni devils. She cannot most likely find anyone to advise or correct her whether her work meets the Sharīʿah guidelines or not; since the man (given that the Sharīʿah guidelines are applied) is far from her workstation, and if she were to be nearby, he would shy away from talking to her in most cases despite that it is allowable.

---

[53] - Recorded by Al-Tirmidhī: (1173).

[54] - Recorded by ibn Khuzaymah: (1685), ibn Hibbān: (5598), and authenticated by al-Albānī in as-Ṣaḥīḥah: (2688).

It was narrated that Abū Hurayrah (رَضِيَ اللَّهُ عَنْهُ) met a woman who was wearing perfume and heading for the Masjid. He said:

أَيُّمَا امْرَأَةٍ خَرَجَتْ مِنْ بَيْتِهَا مُتَطَيِّبَةً تُرِيدُ الْمَسْجِدَ ، لَمْ يَقْبَلِ اللهُ عَزَّ وَ جَلَّ لَهَا صَلَاةً حَتَّى تَرْجِعَ فَتَغْتَسِلَ مِنْهُ غُسْلَهَا مِنَ الْجَنَابَةِ .

"O maid-servant of the Compeller, where are you heading?" She said: "To the Masjid." He said: "And have you put on perfume for that?" She said: "Yes." He said: "I heard the Messenger of Allāh (صَلَّى اللَّهُ عَلَيْهِ وَسَلَّمَ) say:

'Any woman who puts on perfume then goes out to the Masjid; no prayer will be accepted from her until she returns and takes a bath like that of major impurity (perfectly).'"[55]

However, due to the increasing ill-intentions and the fear of the occurrence of unfortunate incidents, men were

[55] - Recorded by ibn Mājah: (4002), Ahmad in al-Musnad: (12/311), and authenticated by al-Albānī in 'Jilbāb al-Mar'ah al-Muslimah': (131).

distant from advising women except in certain circumstances. Consequently, the only one left to advise the woman[56] surrounded by an unlimited number of temptations is her fellow women. They are the ones who are charged with advising and guiding her.

---

56 - **Translator's note:** He refers to the woman whose work is located outside her house.

THE CONCLUSION

There are some results that can be concluded from this research about the woman and her role in offering advice. These results are summed in the following points:

1- The woman is the partner of the man, and she is as responsible for offering advice for others especially her fellow women as the man.

2- Her fulfillment of this role of advice is full of benefits since the Shaytān has sneaked his way towards many women due to their negligence of advice.

3- A woman, by nature, is influential, which is a strong motivation for the righteous women to seize such golden opportunity.

4- Advice is not limited to be offered by mothers only but rather a full spectrum of women. However, each has its own context and circumstances.

5- Not only a woman should offer advice in her house or her guardian's house but also outside them; be that in her study place, workplace, local Masjid and in all of the places she goes.

6- If women were to adhere to the principle of advice in accordance with the guidelines of the Sharīʿah, corruption and immorality would remarkably decrease among them.

7- It is a must to heed one of the earlier examples of the mothers of believers and righteous women mentioned in this research.

The last of our speech is all praise is due to Allāh, the Lord of the worlds.[57]

---

57 - This research has been submitted in the conference of 'advice' which took place in the al-Imām Muḥammad ibn Saʿūd Islāmic university in Riyāḍ at 27-28th day of Muharram 1434 A.H.